Drive the World in a Taxicab

Drive the World in a Taxicab

John Milkereit

LITERARY PRESS
LAMAR UNIVERSITY

ISBN: 978-1-942956-60-0
Library of Congress Control Number: 2018955255

Lamar University Literary Press
Beaumont, Texas

Acknowledgments

I am grateful to the editors of the following journals, chapbooks, and anthologies in which some of these poems first appeared.

Bearing the Mask: Southwestern Persona Poems
Big River Poetry Review
di-verse-city, (various anthologies)
Houston Poetry Festival anthology
Home & Away
Paying Admissions
San Pedro River Review
Swirl
The Untameable City: Poems on the Nature of Houston

During my time in the Rainer Writing Workshop MFA program, I was blessed with three wonderful mentors: Lola Haskins, Kevin Clark, and Greg Glazner. They have challenged me in ways I didn't think were possible. The work presented here is better because of their thoughtful comments. Kevin Goodan also read this manuscript as a faculty adviser. After I made changes, he reviewed it again. Various students in the M.F.A program offered critical insight on some of these poems during our workshop sessions at residencies. Chelsey Clammer made valuable editorial comments on the initial creative thesis and on the final copy.

Poets in the Loop is my monthly critique group that has provided valuable comments on other poems. Thank you Dom, Winston, Chuck, Mary, Kelly, Carrie, Vanessa, Varsha, and Elina. I am also grateful to all the participants of the San Miguel Poetry Week who provided critical insight on this work.

For taxicab drivers and their passengers

CONTENTS

Driving into Waked Water

Dancing From the Seams

Climbing These Makeshift Walls

Keeping Sunrays Out

Driving into Waked Water

Ode to an Outboard Motor inside a Restaurant

Happy hour by the glass
after five o'clock on Sunday
at the Rainbow Lodge as I
look down the hallway
at a weathered end table
behind the caramel candles
next to pussy willows lit up
and see you clamp to
my memory, your squared-off
maroon fuel tank,
when my father and I went
trolling in Lake Ontario,
our lines buried in waked
water, noise and gasoline,
the years gone now after catching
nothing, as cold air takes hold
outside like a big hook
that begins to grasp dusk
in February and I can hear
my father say *don't snag the line—*
another adventure without you,
me just standing on rocks
reeling in time with my fake worm
dragging the bottom of Indian Lake
furious with knotted line
around the reel when I say
I'm never going to fish again—

as I sip pinot noir
from Sonoma, the foggy window
reminds me that your aunts and uncles
were at that lake too
water rippled with laughter at me
through their propellers

so I walked back to my grandparents
house, mowed grass that stood
like the sober faces entering the bar,
bright and slick until the blades cut.

von Fürstenberg

I want to show you
her happy face.
Nose up, ear revealed,
left arm above her head,
the champagne flute held in her hand but not there.
I want to show you the spackled road,
dry pines, drab grass, the sun divided.
I want to show you because you'll want to go
        to Connecticut.
This woman, moistened lips, long black gown,
white straps across shoulders, departed
black strips from hips.
Your face is what you have.
You walk your own road,
wear your own dress,
flowing.

Self-Portrait in Orange

I feel so distant from you when I drive over
mandarin cones that mark off asphalt
at the Rainbow Lodge. The valet says,
"You park across the street for self-park."
This is behind a Japanese Koi bricked house.
"Didn't you see the sign over here?" He points
his index finger towards drab, nestled bushes.
"No, how do I see that sign?" I need a pill,
but I cool off after the valet says it's *okay*.
Inside, the bartender with her mandarin-orange face
pours me a glass of Sonoma wine half-priced.
Sonoma is mandarin orange. Why is it called
the Rainbow Lodge? I see orange-iced lanterns,
the deck lights—Japanese Koi. I imagine orange fish
swimming around here because now I'm outside
on a deck. I don't know why the air conditioning unit
is on, its orange-iced air, loud and unforgiving.
The fish in their Japanese Koi jackets are getting a little
colder since I'm getting cold. Orange is not cold.
Orange is bright mandarin orange, juicy, peeled,
and succulent. Juice is a vitamin, a vitamin is not cold,
even though it's earth-colored. Earth is not orange ice
or mandarin orange. More like a hand that receives warmth
from your hand. When our hands touch, I taste orange
in a pond we swim to as far away as Japan.

Hyde Park

This afternoon after school I'm at the grocery store co-op,
winter outside, hot air already blown up through
a large metal grate at the entrance, my feet insulated
in boots with orange Roman Meal bread bags, to find
laid-back Sam in the meeting room waiting downstairs
in a wool suit, not smoking a cigarette, his stare turned to
me, ready for my first job where I would stamp mahogany
burl stock certificates and stuff them using fingertip
moistener and fold them shut in envelopes using a wet
sponge on glued flaps, then dial the date on the mailing
machine as Edith, another accountant, asked in a baritone
voice from her mustached mouth, "Da ya want something
sweet?" knowing she just opened with her large brown
hand a drawer containing Tootsie Rolls, and who knows
what else, just before I started to run the postage meter,
red ink smelling close to alcohol, clear but often smudged
like Sam's supervision, then the timecard punched clean
on payday. Walking home, I would have enough money
to buy a silver tie clip at Breslaur's for my father.

Race around the World

Dear Sarah:

I know you're going crazy inside that ping-pong ball
called the South Pole. The white sky, the terrain, though you
have your telescopes. I blew you a kiss across our living room.
I hope you win the ten-minute shower because what can
you do with two 2-minute showers a week? How do you
measure time anyway? There is nothing scientific to prove
it even exists, but I don't need to tell you. You're
the researcher. We made heat before you left, and now
you're gone to measure thermal radiation. Can't wait
to run trails with you again. Wear a Lycra suit, and I'll
envelope you in sequins. Tie your keys to your shoelaces.
I promise not to bark about the jingling. I have to admit
I feel dumb in the winter. I sit at my desk all day and sharpen
pencils like Jethro did when he got a job at the bank.
Did you ever watch *The Beverly Hillbillies*? Only I'm not
the sharpener, I'm the pencil with not much of an eraser
because I have to rid myself of everything bad
so I can get better. And run steamy with you rather than
without. Do you *comprende*? If you're ninety degrees south
of the equator running around that airplane runway,
then celebrate in every time zone. Study until your lenses break.
It doesn't take a brain surgeon to know we're getting warmer.
Shave with the water on, okay? Don't let your strides sink
in the snow. Don't let us evaporate.

Fondly,
John

Ansel Adams' Plastic Beach Scene

In the gallery of my own delicate universe,
this scene isn't like a moonrise at Hernandez
or a wintery rock formation
but a Frisbee that leaches across a darkened sky
saucer-like.
The chair backs have gigantic
faces holding people alive, not under tiny
crosses. The backs would be aquamarine and watermelon
if the image were in color,
and they are conversing, spading over words,
some sort of recycled talk, holding water bottles
that look like silos ready to spill water across a glacier
of sand. Sticks are torches rather than birches,
and vehicles are toys parked next to the newest
monument of my father's creation—a turtle.
The backdrop is a freighter carrying
several thousand milk jugs. Pelicans
bend and shatter the surface catching fish
that are as fake as a rose on driftwood—
a package I can't unzip, but I sense is contained
in an inlet of imagination as murky as gelatin—
at least that's my current tide,
that's what I see.

Red Rountree

You never knew, Faye, that after our fifty-year
and one-month love affair, I robbed banks

not as prayers for your return from lung cancer,
but to feel good, awfully good, sometimes for days,

sometimes for hours. My first craving
was in Corpus Christi where that bank

yanked my loan to build oil supply boats
after I had already bought the steel. The unpaid

boats forced my bankruptcy, but I sold refurbished winches salvaged
from warships for oil rigs, and what followed was a ton of money.

Remember how we laughed and hollered like the first day
we met in Freer at that honky-tonk?

When you passed on, I went crazy. Literally crazy.
I smoked marijuana, even tried cocaine.

The arrest of a new gal's hug,
and her two kids I loved to death didn't help

especially when we married and I spent five hundred grand
on her rehab. Honey, the banks, the bars, they broke me.

Social Security held as much money at my age
as an empty manila envelope stenciled in red ink with *Robbery*.

"Are you kidding?" the youngest teller asked twice after
my demand for small bills at the First American Bank

in Abilene. "No, hurry up or you will get hurt," I said.
She complied, I knew she would.

Then, I kicked it up to 90 miles-per-hour in my Buick Regal
with a full tank of gas.

Sylvia

I'm your waitress who used to orbit
on roller skates, drink champagne splits
with a footnote of cherry juice

under dim spotlights. I still train—
nobody else has wheels for this job.
The trainees, they last a day

or maybe longer to chart a course
on whether to dance instead. Hidalgo
is the manager underneath a suit,

a rubble pile, half empty space, paid
a fraction by pimps. If you are a pack rat
millionaire, I'll clean your house

on Saturdays. I custom-make purses
from cigar boxes emptied at Spec's.
I can design Marilyn Monroe

or the hidden compartment. It's like growing
pot in your garage. Who ever said I was a saint?
I've made a bonfire of penis bouquets

for boutiques or a foot-long
member for my husband
when he visits the club

as Santa Claus after I decorate
for nothing with boughs of holly.
I'm on a collision course to retire

on Florida beachfront property.
I'm skin held together by gravity. My hip
is no good even after two injections.

This tray is too heavy. If you recall,
I'm finished with tequila shots, so let's
go eat breakfast one day after we close.

Dear M—

Dear music, dear Madison,
dear memory, this is Southwest Flight 563
to Chicago. I dance with an imaginary friend
in July (a month with no *m*) and she leads
waving her napkin. I think of all the water
to drink in July, all the bicycled parks
with their bluegrass concerts, picnics
with plastic-lettered, assigned cups.
When does a month end? When will
concrete end in Houston and submit to
wild-fed grass? Hiking along the south rim
of the Grand Canyon, I remember how
rock folded open like creases in my hand,
lines of sandstone, and sea-creature limestone
with clots of snow. Dear tambourine,
dear fragile decade, I feel lost in melody
during the summers, almost like a heat stroke,
rare sharks migrating the Gulf, the humidity
dull as a bad blade, the house siding apologetic
with a cracked grin. Where is Frank Sinatra
on New Year's Eve (the tickets were a gift
from my father to my mother), the buckskin Vista Cruiser
driven? My mother wore a white dress
with purple flowers until Angela, our cat, pissed
on it. Where is the kitchen window pelted that night
by a BB gun? Where is the stolen raccoon coat,
the thief's ear print dusted on the front door?
Where is Marilyn Lord, the babysitter who claimed
she was the daughter of Jack Lord, the actor
from *Hawaii Five-O*? Do months end like TV shows,
like waves suspended that eventually ferment
into bubbles? But some months come on
and never stop shouting. Dear mercury, dear mystery,
and To Whom It May Concern: thank you
for not letting my fingers slip into History's waiting glove.

I am not in a diary, not in my great-grandfather's photograph
of Amelia Earhart, the woman who flew into the ocean,
only God knows where, as though there were a string
and she were a bird. History flew a bird that was
calling and calling.

Ode to the Smoked Oyster

The soft fleshy
oyster
snap-shuttered
lived in a
villa
stemmed sideways
invincible
drawing water
over its gills
exchanging gases across mantles
surrounded by ruffled algae.
Above, plankton floating
trapped in mucus
while the oyster waits
until one day
raked
into a pile
our oyster is christened
for duty.
Men ship it out with the others
on parade
towards
docks, iced boxes.

But wait,
here is
John
searching in the back of a liquor store.
He selects, not the sardines
swimming above in their
mustard, but our oyster, now heated
with cherry wood.
He inspects the compact
housing,

eyes the pull-tab.
He pays for it
along with garlic and herb cheese spread,
a box of whole wheat crackers,
and a bottle of whipped-cream vodka.

The Comfort Inn
with its indoor pool
whose children
are too young for Marco Polo
and the unlit, desk lamp broken
in his room.

And here's
the tale of
the shelled body,
we call oyster.
Now smoked,
submerged in virgin oil
I unfurl it
and eat
the thin-walled vessel
of its three-chambered heart.

Dancing From the Seams

Avocado

The plan was to eat half an avocado
with an omelet, but I began by plucking
leaves off cilantro stems over the sink,

forgot I placed the avocado
to ripen in a used coffee bag from Mexico
instead of uncovered on top of the refrigerator,

and that is why I also washed the baby-
bella mushrooms from a cardboard carton
stored near the red peppers in the crisper drawer.

What egg fantasy would not be complete
without heating extra virgin olive oil?
I asked the stove top, but she said nothing,

and so I chopped organic green onions
clipped on their ends
and even cubed a slice of ham

heated and flipped in the Teflon terrain
of my skillet, my spatula
frenzied in the induction-readied arena.

Sorry, avocado, I even forgot
your history when you were called *alligator pear*
or even worse by the Aztecs

lost in the scoop of a bigger forest.
Forgive my middle-aged eyes for overlooking
your precious model

of self-containment from your make-shift
habitat and for not realizing the maturity you've reached—
the bumpy exterior now slightly giving in

and your flesh underneath bright green
available on a board waiting
for the rapid, undeniable dive of the spoon.

Commemorative Stamps

hibernate in a cardboard box. At twelve
I am driven in and out of a new kind
of hormone, the kind where you get off collecting,
private walks to the post office, making sure
to breathe before licking a hinge to a page
in the album you earn after modeling clothes
for a Marshall Field's catalog. Other stamps
thread behind thin, glossed windows that picture
granite from mountains, jawbones of presidents,
a block of butterflies, horses racing past
the last turn. I crack open the album at dusk
under my Beach Boy haircut before setting
the dinner table to see how many pages
I had to fill. What I wanted was to feel whole.
How could I have imagined then how alone
I would become with their value?

The Great American Sandwich

If this were a streetcar,
you would begin with passengers,
a man alone reading a book
or a young woman looking from a window.

As wheels squealed, you would realize
that it was an afternoon on St. Charles Avenue
or a late night after drinking Hurricanes at Patty O's,
and I would describe the street-named tiles

on the sidewalk and what the man was reading,
even the chapter shown on the opaque page,
and the seersucker jacket he folded onto his lap,
as well as the live oaks flanked past his view.

If one can only wait so long, you would know
where the streetcar was taking the man
or further details of the woman's neighborhood,
and you would not have the patience to see

the streetcar empty downriver or have any desire
to see the man relish his walk like a naked light bulb
to the loud poker party or that the woman was headed
to replace her kitchen candle with a paper lantern.

But this is a poem about a po' boy.
We are the only characters involved
in our own Big Easy which will end
after swallowing the lettuce and last tomatoes,

preventing us from having a fistfight
or the energy to swim across river to Gretna.
Will juice from a hot mess eventually
run down your arm, or how must bread

not overwhelm the rest of the sandwich?
Like how do we feel after eating every last
flaky crumb? We hunger for rides better than
all the streetcars that could deliver us to ruin.

A Community of Coffee Mugs
for John E. Walsh

Precariously stacked,
       they are upside
down in the cupboard
with ceramic surfaces
       keeping hot from cold
with pictures reminding us
       where time ebbed on.

Sailors coast along
       the beige sea of the cabinet,
or hold ropes above
the foam-capped dishwasher waves.

After hours of confinement, I wonder
if the Mickey Mouse mug would order
Van Gogh's *The Starry Night* to shift its centerline
or yell at *Café Du Monde* for more beignets on deck.
Would Jefferson's *Monticello* declare independence?
Or does *Kiawah Island* search for the sands of vacation?
The *Banibel Blue* and *Banibel Green* stoneware
whispers they will stay onboard despite *Sooo Bitchen*,
whose language causes morale problems.
And what exactly would *The Caffeine-Meister, The Beanster*,
with his slicked-back hair and peach-colored sock tie
say about the quality of the java juice?

Each morning, one of them travels upstairs
treading along the walnut grains of my desk
and washes upon the shore of a white paper napkin
to catch its breath.

Each of them exhales a story
       I say
as my lips touch their edges,
as my palms feel their weight,
sip after sip awakening me
openmouthed.

Letter to Holman

Dear Rick:

I wanted to mention at the grocery store the other night
that I almost took a blonde to Hawaii. Since then I've been miserable.
It's nothing like what you're going through with Monica. Her cerebellum
is shrinking—there's nothing you can do. I'm reaching an age where
I can't get women. Still, you had your blonde. And a son, a daughter.
I can help with the cistern. I can design pipe to deliver rainwater
with a pump and a motor. You're going to make that house
on four acres. The Big Island—your fifth trip. Amazing, on the coast
with dolphins. You build the way you want. Will never replace Monica,
but you decide what goes inside, not God. I want to date this young
Hawaiian girl. Though I'm older than her father. But none of them
are young, you know? As you said, we're rehearsing bad theater.
You say your lines because you're a lawyer. I can't.
When did an engineer ever nail a line? The worst thing is
Monica knows what to say but can't. She acts drunk. I'm still sorry
your house burned down on Thanksgiving. Did you find Socks?
Your artwork is gone. Christ, your garden. On a good day, I took
that blonde to Napa and rode the wine train. Drove a convertible
south to Carmel. Build that house. Capture the pink cloud shapes.
Love your rainfalls.

Your friend,
John

Memorandum

Date: *July 9*
To: *Lab Technicians*
From: *Edward Watkins, Section Head*
Re: *Drug Trail Status*

I want to make this super-clear about the Wildwood Project.
One way is to do the job poorly with a negative attitude.
Say we need to clean the sauna. If we spend an hour before
sauna-cleaning bad-mouthing the process of cleaning the sauna,
screwing around with kitchen utensils, jacking off in a towel,
so what, what occurs next is that we make the process of cleaning
the sauna *more infinitely harder than it appears*. We all know
those saunas have to be cleaned, given that you have to fuck
in the sauna, or by the next Joe or Joette if your washing skills
suffer, so my question is: Do I clean it with a happy face or do I clean it
with a sad face? What would make my stay here more purposeful?
What is my mission? To avoid going back to jail. What mood do I bring
to clean the sauna sparkly and rapidly? Bad? A bad mood state?
What I'm saying is we need to make these trials of this sex drug work.
Where? Outside in the thin cosmic cool air?
You know well the answers. The point of the memo is: Happy.
The happy mental state will assist you in cleaning the sauna,
so doing it bunny-happy in the sauna happens, steamy or not,
thus finishing this trial and your mission of a shortened sentence.

Ed

Wednesday Dollar Dog Night

Just before you eat the hot dog
there is the glimpse,
a flush of Nolan Ryan Beef,
not skinnier, less weighty
than regular nights,
and the body continues to
plump, cooks on roller grills
after you resist the chicken waffle cone,
or the Bloody Mary with a floating
slice of cold pizza, or a deep-fried,
bacon-wrapped, chocolate-covered mashup
parading like a prostitute at Easter service.
And you're poised before the start of the game
which is really the same game
just advancing from one wiener
to bun to foiled jacket to ketchup
to onion back in foiled jacket to devouring
to blessed watching.
The ball pops the catcher's mitt.
When the home town hits, every home run
is a miracle and the scoreboard lights up.
Fans rise, strangers slapping high-fives
agreeing in the silent voice we all hear:
winning makes us hungry.

On *Marshland*

Gaia,

I want to say it's great to see your mural.
I've climbed Houston trees for no particular reason
for decades. Before moving here, I painted with acrylics.
The canvasses are long gone. I thought of that inside your pineappled
pillars and actually got depressed. I perceive time better
than happy people. The birds came first, and they were trying
to eat red tape? They flew through some government regulations.
Or am I supposed to get a profound sense of pollution?
Maybe that was just me—confused. My sexual desire
is currently suppressed the way Slovakian researchers
did to red flour beetles. The mural's pretty faces redeem me.
Especially the smiling female undergrad student.
I wasn't going to say anything last Saturday, but
all I thought about was sex and what you didn't paint.
Was she wearing a silk dress? I prefer zippers than buttons.
Gaia, you didn't know you make me hungry. Maybe I don't touch
the student. It makes no difference whether I have sex.
I want to sleep with her, but then I don't.
I believe in fairness, but I don't believe in forcing myself
on grayish-blue lines scribbled over peoples' faces. How does Jesus
save those who don't smile? Do you think we announce
our travel plans in advance like male orangutans?
I thought of that. This is really no paraiso scene for the young.
Sorry, I'm getting carried away. But you know, Gaia,
under the bluish skies of migration, how does one dance?
Friction begins in the bayou, behind every black-dotted
piece of glass, and every wedding sari. Doesn't matter if a barn owl
failed to deliver two wedding rings because he fell asleep.
Folks here marry; hump each other just like they do in Baltimore.
The gulf between you and this town is not so wide. Hell, I love
these scenes even if I don't believe they're all true.

Wish you were here drinking a beer with the bikers at this icehouse. The ceviche with tortilla chips is superb.

Best of Luck,
John

Memorandum

December 20, 2014

Given the changing seasons, I would like to review
proper maintenance of the hot oil machines. Part of the job
that we are getting paid to do well for the Wildwood Project
is routine cleaning of the machines. Like removing bundles
and brushing internals of the heating coils. And dispensing oil
and smearing it all over our bodies before it's hot. Not correct.
One way to do the job poorly is to hurry. Or to plum forget. Each staff
member needs to take ownership and not have a negative attitude
about the hot oil machines. Am I being clear? Am I saying we
should hold hands and sing a merry tune every day now?
Maybe I'm saying do whatever it takes. Say we need to protect
a hippopotamus from being eaten alive. Forgive the hippo analogy,
but we just returned from a safari vacation in Botswana
where there were a lot of broken heaters and cold nights
plus a real hippopotamus that was about to be attacked by lions.
Do you think we could have rescued the hippopotamus
with some giant slings and lifted it with a helicopter?
Even if the hippopotamus had a mirror, with bodies
turning as fast as they do, the sudden shadows of lions,
even its own shadow, would it react to save itself in time?
I think you know the answer. We all know a helicopter rescue
would have been difficult. What makes the task more difficult
is being hurried and having a bad attitude.
Even saying: "I don't live in Botswana and why should I care
about the food chain I know nothing about" makes the task infinitely
more difficult than it has to be. We huddled together and made a plan.
To extend the analogy further, everyone had a role to play.
Some helped by lighting torches, others knew how to shoot
with a rifle, and another big husky guy knew where to find a truck
to haul the animal away. A group of complete strangers convinced
a hippopotamus that knew none of us to amble onto a truck. Amazing.
What I'm saying is we have to care, right?
The chances of having the best sexual intercourse increase

when the oil is at the optimum temperature, and there's enough oil
because the hot oil machines aren't fouled. If we have our heads
in the proverbial sand and think the machines are going to maintain
themselves, then whom are we kidding? Lions are like the outside
influences in the world that skew results. I can ramble on and on,
but come visit me if you have doubts. Doubting oneself is another killer.
I will show you a video of the hippopotamus and its wide body,
and how she climbed up the ramp of the truck to safety.

What We Said at Brunch

Saturday in Austin—
I see your eyes in my coffee
and your hair in my beef tacos.

You say no brunch and eat yellow
squash. I say ship carrots steaming
across an ocean.

Rose. I forget to tell you
that color. Remember, salsa
is a good source of beta-carotene.

You think rice. Me—
beans. I do not mind the color black.
You say long ago you swore off white.

I am glad you survive
this adventure—escaping the quicksand
of smoothies. Hiking gorges of pancakes.

I am drifting off wondering why
we accept dinner next week
at a steakhouse in Carmine, Texas.

Instead, why not order fish?
I love brown. That baked potato must go,
so we will ask for kale. We debate dessert

like the long-handled fans batted at movies
set in ancient Egypt. We just
leave silent, toward our cars.

Popcorn

We walked to the train station in Hyde Park
for the first of many times to see the Chicago
White Sox, and I ate popcorn, that puffed elegance,
those kernels shaken from the bottom of a pot,
now risen from oil and salt. Just a big grocery bag full,
carried as if our lives depended on its warmth
as we rode to 35th Street. I'll never forget Wilbur Wood,
the first pitcher burned into memory, who threw
a knuckleball that danced from the seams,
fluttered, this white blob riding into the air,
swung over by sluggers' bats. And I won't forget
my father passing the bag between innings
to the nine-year-old boy who reached in
and caught this buttered saltiness which still
arrives between my teeth
and leaves after I drink a cold beer.

Ice Cream Love Song

Come lick with me, be my candylicious junkyard,
and we'll scoop some cashew brick
where fingers, lips, tongues, teeth,
eyes, even a luscious mouth lingers.

And we'll snuggle around lemon velvet
watching the young girls dip their truffles
near the really rocky road for they're all
raspberry chiffons off to dance at malty balls.

And I'll stuff kooky cookie dough
plus a million nutter butters
chase one shot of espresso, and bit
a ribbon full of midnight decadence.

A dress cut from the krispy rice treats
where the sugar fields we once cropped;
brownie-supreme shoes strut the floor
with heels teddy high in cin grahams.

A buckle of creamy dreamy and cherries
with ample pecans and marshmallows,
so if these delights make you turn,
come lick with me, be my candylicious junkyard.

The girls will swing and laugh
because they smile every orange sunrise.
If those smiles pretzel hips, make you turn,
come lick with me, be my candylicious junkyard.

Memorandum

June 21, 2015

    We were supposed to meet outside the workplace
of the Wildwood Project to review the decline of the numbers
before summer begins. The absences I excused were because of the rain,
flash flooding, and fear of drowning in a car. Yet when I said this
at the Divisional Meeting, I didn't get one iota of sympathy. The smirks
from upper management were brutal. I mean brutalizing. And now
here I am, at this restaurant, to discuss why the saunas have gone
unclean which skews the ability to perform the acts we have to commit
with the drugs. However, no one else is here due to inclement weather?
The weather people with their stupid salaries based on reporting chaos.
The rain is in Matagorda Bay now if you believe the latest news,
and I know none of you live around Matagorda Bay, so what will
your excuse be this time? I'm drinking a hoppy beer here listening to
another idiotic love song off satellite radio by that ex-surfer,
Jack Johnson. I'm concerned that we're going down a path
of self-doubt that could be suicidal. Has anyone ever sprayed
with a power-washer? I know a few of you did at Dick's house.
Isn't it invigorating to hold down on the trigger, at the risk of numbing
your finger, and watch the water hammer again and again on his siding?

    What am I saying? I'm saying become friends with water again.
Hammer hard at your assigned tasks, cleaning away the grit
and mold of a bad attitude, which will result in a happy face.
I've seen great sex in the saunas from so many of you
especially in the record-setting month of April that caused
so many positive reverberations. Some of you even planted
Indian paintbrush and blue bonnets in the dirt plot
in front of our building. So close the seeds probably
cross-pollinated. Setting aside the current dark mumbo-jumbo feelings,
weren't we having fun in April? God, we hammered away
by cleaning with jet water, hammered hard against each other,
which burned smithereens of calories. Wasn't it a site to see

the flurry of bodies chasing after clean towels? I saw joy
on your sweat-beaded faces.

Ed

Climbing These Makeshift Walls

I Am Upset That Residents of Gaza Are Still Waiting for Cement to Repair Their Homes After Fear It Will Be Used for Military Purposes

This cement has committed no crimes, you know?

No cement is walking like a donkey strapped with
explosives. Cement in a bag does expire.

Cement doesn't make the artillery shell
that is discourteous to someone's wall, not really,
doesn't stop a carnation blossom, doesn't seal
the border shut. Now even flowers can't be exported,
so they're just bouquets to feed sheep.

So please, let's not be scared of cement.

No cement wished for tunnels,
ever wanted to live in a warehouse.
This cement is a friend and should be granted
to fix one room in an apartment. What
is this wait we assign when those that suffer
can't have any cement?

People deserve better than plastic sheets for walls.

This cement doesn't ask for a happy job.
It has not been waiting to dance with its body
half-hidden near the market.

Remembering Joel Shapiro's *New Installation*

What will become of all the wood
       hung in the gallery cut from spruce
eyehooks screwed into sloped grains
             that purple cube hoisted like Fat Tuesday
       the wind-yelped cords of yellow wheat
the tequila-knotted lime 2 x 4
one end of green and orange imploded
       towards center, thoughts unconstrained
in space like the almost forgotten naughty night
          the unpainted coffin is forever flesh
      violet supersaturated the back ceiling
and the blood-scorched door that closed,
          in this room white and strung up.

Disclaimers on Reading

Good evening,
I need a glass of water.
Sorry that I'm late.
Where is the microphone?
The traffic is horrible and did you know
twenty-three alcohol-related deaths have occurred
near this intersection in the past two weeks?
I was not informed there would be a duct-taped
brass-plated, music stand instead of a podium.
Why is there a dartboard behind my head?
I never received notification of the five-minute time
allotment of the re-enforcement with flash card
warnings and hand waving SOS signals.
Why not turn off the televisions so no one can watch
"Monday Night Football?"
I am hallucinating from antibiotics and had planned
to arrive with 24-font bold until my printer died.
Why does the waitress continue to clang the plates
and clink the pint glasses?
I would rather eat dinner now, have a decent night of sleep,
or walk next door and fantasize over the breath-of-fire
yoga position.

But there is not enough time,
                my budget has been obliterated.
The chances of having my requests fulfilled are hopeless.
Every cost estimate of repairing my situation is at least
50% more than the cost of starting over again.
The risk of lung cancer is beyond my control,
so due to ongoing environmental concerns,
I must vacate the premises
once the cigarette smoke clears
and I see the exit sign near the mounted
deer antlers.

                Thank you.

Hygge

after Renata Lucia's *Hygge*

The word
means a coziness for the soul

As if
renting a bicycle in Copenhagen
and pedaling for porridge comforts life

Five letters of yarn and thread
balanced on the handlebars

Its crocheted position
undeniably unrevealed
between *Hygeia* and *hygiene*
words spun in Webster's dictionary

The absolute act
of art
sewn
to send across the Atlantic

This touch of revelation

Vignettes of letters
shrilled by colorful flowers
for a bouquet of reflections

This assemblage
of stacked nourishment
quilted fabric
as spotlights
strike
its body

Hunkering down
for a tropical storm's landfall
washes this creation
into a gorgeous silence

Work for Joy

What face will I wear today?
I want a simple smile like the one
in Alexander Calder's sculpture—
the copper wire head and ears,
threaded clear glass eyes,
and the reflector red mouth hung
from a broken blue nose that looks thirsty.
I like this work when I do not need a drink.
Right now the cafeteria is closed, so I will
not smile at this sculpture or him. And I
am mad at his bird made from a coffee can body
and a beer can beak. I blew on the cans when
the guards were not looking to prove someone
emptied them in the air currents, and no one
explained who drank all the coffee or the beer.
I wish he had propelled an apology
to those who see his work that are unhappy
with thirst.

Sifted

after Smucker's relocation of the White Lily flour mill

Don't take my soft red winter
away, exactly where you won't say
but if it's north, where protein lives,
the enemy of light would crust open,
and I would awaken as a blended
variety that yields less to high
rise.

I don't need your knead either
in darkened kitchens, in deep pans
swallowing time for pizza dough
caked in too much sauce. Stop
the ritual of smothering meat kings,
mozzarella crowns, and mushroomed
jewelry. No, I'm way too ground
down and choked on olive oil.

Keep the oven heated though.
I'm tucked for warmth, cut-in,
soaring, blue-ribboned, weightless,
and blown from underneath
the husk of the bran layer.
Embrace me. Harvest the purest
germ.

In the Cubicle

We labor in our cubicles, typing,
handling manila folders like littered bottles
from damp grass, envelopes for payroll:
owlishly scary.
Backs bent forward in our chairs,
we are clay and toothpick, stooped,
over our desks like Edgar Degas' ballerinas
at the Paris Opera, though maybe more repressed
here, work that encourages us to file our nails,
lemon-flavored vodka *for people who need*
people and the peaceful getaway to San Benito.
We love our chocolate cake and extreme
action figurines, a drug test from home—
the marijuana we have grown in our garages
like long-ago teenager boys.
Time is lost at 11:12 a.m. even though
we quickly age under a grid
of fluorescent lights, a loss of motivation,
without movement in a normal place,
taping photos of our orange-faced family
on a cabinet ready for the cosmos,
purified by chugging water, which stops
us from reading the latest clipped-out
cartoon. We know our stuff is fed into
a mechanical winch by cables in a way
that without us, this place will become a zone
of disaster by December. The phius plant, once potted,
has already been yanked, fallen on the carpet
like an old woman on uneven cellar stairs.
We can climb over these makeshift walls,
growing stronger from the chalkboard
we erased just yesterday, causing us to smile
at each other, our hopes piled as high as the paper.

Disgruntled Tree

after Mary Temple's light installation
Northwest Corner, Southeast Light

No, you cannot take my picture for the gazillionth
time or the greatest of insults paint shadows

on the wooden floor so you can trick
people with bottle-nosed psychology

and who really cares about a sense of equilibrium.
I hate magnolias but you know that even though

I'm your neighbor in Central Park
and they're from a Houston temple

which seems like I'm on an Ouija board
not a wall so don't think I'm calm after

applying tiny-weensy brushstrokes of sealant
which is the opposite of your title

this swath is the *southwest* corner lady
and light is from the *northeast* direction

of your little *trompe l'oeil*.
I will live longer than you and the carpenters

I will suffer after feeling your nails
and sanding. What about a couple minutes of voir dire

to admit I am smarter than you and your little thing-a-ma-bob
project? I will never visit this gallery again

even though I admit to digging the last exhibit
when the metal-airplane-looking wing jutted

through glass. I will not embrace any more silhouettes.
I hate sucking up to your "not-knowing" confusion

because it is all fake fake fake. I would rather talk
to a yam thanks to you I'm all Alfred Hitchcock now

with the birds but I am not like that.
I lied about the magnolias. I like magnolias

and Dominique de Menil because she hugs
I do not have to pose in your fantastic fantasy
behind a camera if you could just see

with your own naked eyes, it is just so psycho
and sorry. All of this is just really, really sad.

Consolation after Missing Dickens

Joy is walking.
48 Doughty possesses no yard, no flowers.
He only lived here two measly years.
A clock, a pen quill, some silver cufflinks, a silver
cigar clip, a Christmas tree are probably buried behind this door.
He wrote *Nicholas Nickleby* in this house.
I never read *Nicholas Nickleby*.
I inherited silver bowls, ladles, and Christmas tree salt shakers.
Did Dickens have a collection?
The tour book sleeps at the B&B.
How do you ring up 411 in London?
Telephone numbers look like a Sudoku puzzle.
Pip, that *Great Expectations* character, is weird—
he walks around a house with a rotting wedding cake?
If I had to illustrate, I'd find an illustrator. I can't draw.
Why draw?
Who reads fiction in a newspaper?
My bank has called. Fraud is in the fog.
My ATM card is zapped.
Admission price would keep twenty children alive in Zaire
        for years.
Is Dickens buried at the Abbey?
This drudgery to underground darkness
                back to the Tube, back to Chancery Lane
                        is a double-decker of exhaustion.
I want my bones cremated
                my heart protected in a biscuit tin
like Hardy's
        away from clawing
                prying conspiracy theorists
spilt Guinness, and I need a bronze likeness similar to Hodge,
        Samuel Johnson's cat
                holiday-ribboned collar

61

standing erect in Gough Square
                where eyes searched for words, wit,
conversation that ruled the middle of this court's air.

Experiments in Truth

> The problem [is defining] images that illustrate an *aesthetic of nonviolence*. Is there a relationship between nonviolence and truth?—Josef Helfenstein, director of this art exhibition at The Menil Collection

I.   Glock 17
              after seeing Mel Chin's "HOMEySEW 9"

Let's have an agenda
where new mechanics
disarm its aura.

Mill the magazine
as a micro-electronic
locator of the bullet

spring-load the barrel
with normal saline
IV needle and polyethylene

tubing. Pin the chamber
with a fourteen-gauge
angiocatheter

with two-inch elastic
bandage. We'll harden
our model with point

three milligrams of
intramuscular epinephrine
point five milligrams of oxycodone

hydrochloride and
five hundred milligrams of
acetaminophen.

A covert operation
for treating gunshot
wounds from a weapon

originally developed
for the military and
police of Austria

popularized by film,
music, video games
though our life-saving

kit wouldn't have stopped
death at Luby's—
the cafeteria in Killeen

Texas doubtful Gaston
Glock would have been
torn apart if he knew.

II.   A Blind Trial
                    after Robert Gober

Beeswax breasts
have no torso
thrown onto an applewood

chair bottom cast from
gypsum polymer with
olive paint and alabaster

legs fastened to
the gallery wall. Orange
areolas soften by

sight across the aisle
Glock 17. They don't
see a rifle handle below

slender pewter
barrels riding to
back of chair

bottom underside
curling over the lip
boring down

III.   Verification of Light
                    after Dan Flavin

Cherry red
fluorescent tubes
on metal fixtures

are burning
not burnt out for
a young woman

and men unplugged
at Kent State
and Jackson State.

The lights mount cornered
a lime tube
behind like incursion

into Cambodia for
other students
lamps will become

inoperative once
they flicker
troops lamps

do we need more
or just remember

what they gave

given that gun
across the gallery
will last forever

IV.   Tank Man

Skinny slope-shouldered
in this video which is not
a game. White shirt

black trousers he walks in front
of one tank that leads
a column of

tanks rolling along
the yellow stripe
of Cangan Boulevard

the Avenue of Eternal
Peace near a square
where bird-faced kites

soar and peasants from
the countryside gather
only the square is

Tiananmen June fifth
1989 he's waving his plastic
shopping bag at

the tank as if this protest
is an afterthought
the tank still

not listening but
beginning to hear now
he leaps onto the red-starred

hull opens turret hatches
like they are ears
and pleads to

someone
then he climbs down
a brief puff of engine smoke

the tank angles right
he dances in front
unaware tanks are not
dance partners
rather war machines that
crush vehicles and
people like
they did yesterday
tank man's chandeliers

street lamps
with little white globes
and his walls

padded
with green trees and the
Beijing Hotel

a bicyclist and two other men
the Public Security Bureau
who knows

hustle him away
he's sentenced
fourteen days later

or not or living
some curious courage
this fellow

Shotgun

after seeing an exhibit by Atelier Bow-Wow
and the Rice School of Architecture that pays
homage to Houston's historic row houses

Type of house on Lake Houston's shore,
pitched roof over an elongated box,
type of clear path, Igloo next to a dog.

Type of slight cut tied to the 4-Bay Single
and Double. Type of house that is Camelback.
Type of retirement and corridor layout,
tax-enforced with No. 2 pine, robin's egg blue painted
from Leesville, Louisiana, T-shirt on a plastic hangar,
rooster on a wall-mounted A/C unit.

Type of house in shot-thru, ghost light bulb dangling
over the front porch, type of house that pivots
big cozy chairs pulsing through afternoon,
weight-lifting press, clothesline clasping a bed sheet,
clusters of cracked foundations, *Beware of Dog* signs,
potted caladium on a folded chair, nearby Union Pacific
locomotive, white-vested cat on an office chair

with rollers when the Talking Heads sang
"Once in a Lifetime." Type of third- and fifth-ward row,
keep-the-shot, quadruple cabin, sanded split-studio,
tight-block densifying, multi-generational,
woman-standing-over-a-man statue,
no trespassing, hex-head screwed
with Dewalt tools, Bow-Wow hard hats.

Reflections on the New Urban Décor of Paris

after seeing photographs by Charles Marville

I. Lamppost, Entrance to the École des Beaux-Arts, 1870

Armed men
with lanterns are no
longer needed at night

centered is a gas lamp
its face looking regal
four ways no less

above the skinny sidewalk
bordering millstones
of the museum wall

supporting a statue
in the upper right
a man with no arms

arched entrance cut off
trees leafless
egg-whitened by albumen print

II. Rue de Constantine

The view looks toward
the Palace of Justice
before the street was destroyed

a woman is not selling grapes
from a two-wheeled cart
her face smudged out

by shutter speed
men guard holes dug with shovels
hands in their pockets

as if they won't stand
there forever for more rain
the silver rain

makes the horse-drawn
carriages move
unnoticed is the ad

tacked to a dark building
in the lower left corner
for parapluie réductible

the invention for
retractable umbrellas
in the American style

III. Urinal, Jennings System, Plateaude l'Ambigu, 1876

Pissoir!
The stalls are organized
in a ring

shielding the body
from knees to neck
is a metal fence

topped with a street lamp
that says, "For relief
Monsieur, no shame, please"

Prying eyes
see early morning avenues
no clotted chaos

eventually a piercing
and clearing
for new byways

will cause a madame
to stare saucer-eyed
clutching a birdcage

IV. Self-Portrait at a Window, February 20, 1851

The open window—
a casual tumble of light
in focused air

my hand holds a
paper negative which
means French Ministry

no more illustrations
and I will pen you
a letter asking

to take photographs
of your monuments
your art objects

I'm looking out
this frame devoted
to a dry method

the time of exposure
up to fifteen minutes
the time past *Bossu*—

my last name
meant *hunchback*
these troubles, these *ennuis*

jettisoned past time
of Victor Hugo's book
and of my slightness

I'm drawing a new career
ma ville
past this shadowed geometry

How to See Light

In 1664,
     when I was baptized
sixteen years before in March,
I stood by the attic window of our house with my father,
once a tile painter of cupids, children, and fish,
          who glazed, fired, and sold
the tiles until the day of his accident.
     The kiln exploded.
         I saw light touch his face,
            looked where his eyes had been,
     where a doctor sewed shut skin.
"Griet, I can't provide for you any longer—
I did my best," he said.
     "I don't know this man, do you?" I asked.
I would start as a maid
tomorrow in this strange man's house,
     live with him,
     and his family for eight stuivers a day.
"Yes, I do. It's the painter, Vermeer. Johannes Vermeer."
        I remember his painting, a view of Delft
        from the Rotterdam
and Schiedam Gates—the large canvas sky,
long shadows
     in the water,
sand painted in bricks and roofs.

***

I was born in March 1964, and how I wanted to swim in a pool
     or at least stand in a shower
but we have no water in this lava-bricked four-plex.
     I see at this point that I'm no model to paint—
me riding in a brown semi-burned BMW
        owned by my roommate,

who is driving on the wrong side of the road—
no doubt from his days of studying in London.
                              It's January 1986 and a pipe burst.
We agree to shower at the gym
                              and sweat playing racquetball.
He is agile, quick in this game, always wins.
"You need more wrist in the swing, you can't just stand there,"
        he suggests. I feel like a moose with no rack gripping a racket.
He is studying metallurgy
        often up late nights with an electron microscope.
I'm earning an engineering degree.
                  We work crossword puzzles at the kitchen table
and watch *Cheers* on TV.
                  I begin to know about metal on nights before
the red-eyed gym mornings.
                  I learn that an O-ring is not an onion ring greased
at The Varsity often taken in flight by a pigeon's neck.
When O-rings swell,
                or don't bend back
the failure is evident in the clouds above Cape Canaveral.
When a pressurized burning gas
                        impinges propellant
on the aft field joint,
                    O-rings fail at low temperature.
I'm in Atlanta failing
                a physics final exam today
as Christa McAuliffe ascends.
                    Metal bent away, the gap
opening I learn is called *joint rotation.*
                    Pressure is the anti-agent of NoDoz,
and Mello Yello.
Stress is white metal,
                    inelastic rubber,
scarecrow blood.

***

I'm turning around like a bird in flight, not cheerful,
                    trying to find my apron, caps, a prayer book,
and a tortoiseshell comb—
                    a shell shape too elegant for a maid.
I might fail my new master who wants his studio cleaned
                    without moving anything.
An easy enough task to perform for my blind father,
                    no small duty for a painter that sees.
                              I buy raw meat and fish.
I launder daily. I am tired.
        Soap and water crack my hands,
steam reddens my face.
                    The iron is not kind on my arms.
                    "It is called a camera obscura," he says one day.
I'm nervous to see under a robe
                    but when I see through the glass
fixed underneath, the woman
in the painting is missing.
                    The pewter basin, the yellow curtain in the corner,
and the powder-brush remain brighter, clearer.
                    "What color are the clouds?" he asks
as I look out the window another day.
        "White, sir."
"Are you positive?"
                    After I glance further, "And grey
        like the inside of an oyster shell,
yellow like the onions, green like turnips."
        "Yes, you see there is no pure white in clouds,
                              but people claim
they are white."

***

I glance at clouds on the other side of a window
                    as dark as the outside of an oyster shell.
I'm no longer in Atlanta sweating
                    for showers and failing physics.

It's now 2007, and my therapist says with his brushed white hair,
                    "It's about self-esteem."
I combust inside
                    the contours of a chair with armrest
upholstery almost like touching a pearl.
"You link yourself by the evaluation of others."
The air in the office reminds me how I blocked myself
from seeing red after visiting
                    a woman in Savannah on Valentine's Day.
                         All shades of red: carmine, chili pepper,
cheating cherry cheesecake.
                    "And then you're out of time.
Get this disorder remedied
                    by the time you're fifty," he continues.
Like my tank has been running full
                    on bad gasoline I pumped
at the convenience store *Starvin' Marvin*.
                    "It's about reshaping how you see."

***

I could not stop seeing.
                    Light shone on a pitcher was not white
but other colors.
"Now I would like you to make black paint, Griet," he said.
          With a muller, I took my stance at grinding
a piece of charred ivory.
"Keep turning your shoulder, finish with your wrist," he ordered.
The next day, I learned how to grind white lead
then madder and massicot.
                    I washed away impurities
rinsing and re-rinsing
                    to remove chalk or gravel.
The following year he painted me in ocher and lead-tin yellow.
I tied his lady-blue cloth around my forehead,
                    wound a lady-yellow piece
covering my crown.

I did not wear the color of a maid: brown.
When he finished, a brightness was missing.
Before he knew what was needed,
before I bought a bottle
of clove oil to numb the ear,
and chose the thinnest needle and flamed the tip,
before the lobe would swell,
before he borrowed his wife's pearl earring
from the wife he never painted,
I knew my end would be near,
but I came free.

Before I Start Reading This

You should know words connected here
form a sort of surprise.

Not to say too much, but a sideways
Mount Kilimanjaro is revealed on the page
in a high altitude way I hope you'll enjoy.
It's what the known is blowing in your face.

For what you don't know, I brought a boom box.
The second stanza is a humpback whale recorded
from a satellite over the Indian Ocean. Language
is so buoyed. Did anyone bring an extension cord?

When the yellow wheat fields are mentioned,
sway your arms back and forth.
Pretend you're in Kansas. I hope
you didn't want a metaphorical moon. Just howl.

Are you familiar with a pork chop in every
Guinness? It's hidden.

And Merwin is just Merwin, Snodgrass is,
you know Snodgrass, and Collins is just
Judy. The singer.

Actually Snow White never had stepmothers.
They were just mothers.

That mountain is actually a Fibonacci valley
of Times New Roman dripping with carbon monoxide.
You know where the dirty gas comes from.

I forgot to mention I've never read here before.
Or anywhere. Let me just say I brought two poems.
This is the shorter one. And I wrote them today.

Nine Ways of Looking at My Absurd Palace

after Thorsten Brinkmann's art installation,
The Great Cape Rinderhorn

I   A dream on a far-off island—a perfect place to live.
    The journey takes 120 days in a canoe carrying
    sticky jars with gadgets in water.

II   An assemblage of armor for idiots.
    Its front is a wooden shipping crate. It, like us, has a fragile
    side pointing up. It is not real estate to sing with feathers
    perching in the soul.

III   Living inside out. Clothes drape
    over a secret crawl space. The drab-green sofa
    and coffee table relocate to the front patio. He tacks on nature's wall
    the larger photographs and a spare box spring mattress.

IV   A movie of a king with a cape
    and a white bucket over his head. Gumballs are 25 cents
    each, but there are no more gumballs.

V   The land is barren with crops.
    A knight rides into foliage of tacky
    wallpaper to find the Holy Grail. He returns with a gigantic
    horn to bless the palace for good harvest.

VI   "Why was there a recall of all the gumballs?" asks my absurd palace.
    "My life is like Frankenstein's."

VII   Dolly Parton plays in his bedroom on 8-track.
    Kenny Rogers or Tom T. Hall sings at night.
    On the nightstand, a horse trots.

VIII Tangerines grow from a palm tree.

IX   A woman has a shamrock on her neck.
      She is probably bad luck because the rest of herself
      is a belt vibrator exercising machine.

Workshop

I'm sorry to submit
this poem. You don't have time
before Monday for this.
Your imagination won't seed
north of Tupelo, a town where
this poem forgot it lived on a street
that had the sounds of esses.
However, I'm submitting it to you.
The knife can't make this
more dull.

I know you read a couple
thousand poems a year.
Plus memoirs and fiction.
Did you know the woman sitting
next to me cast
my work to the bottom
of the gulf?

My poem is a catfish.

I'm really sorry.
I hope you don't read anything into this.

I gutted most of the stanzas.
I dropped a puppy in the middle.
I machete lines and the remains
formed a haiku about a tarantula
or at least a tarantula shape.

This doesn't mean I'm ignoring
comments from the last workshop
that rejected this poem—which I enjoyed.

This poem has Alzheimer's.
I know you didn't want me to attend.
Think of me as the placebo.
Or a trial case that brings the snacks.

I'll save other poems from myself
and unwrite what is written.
I won't withdraw, no matter what.
And I'm really, very sorry.

Enter My Honeycombed Vault

after Anila Quayyum Agha's art installation, *Intersections*

I remember praying
in Pakistan at home, not the mosque,
discomforted as a woman.
The inspiring Alhambra Palace is like my heart,
        a red castle.

In Pakistan at home, not the mosque,
I didn't know laser-cutting wood would lead us
        to confronting boundaries, pure and knife-edged
as my heart, a red castle like the Alhambra Palace,
its rustled leaves, trickled fountains within, even though

confronting our pure and knife-edged boundaries,
        I didn't know would lead to wood laser-cut.
I couldn't resist wiring a 600-watt light bulb.
Even rustled leaves, trickled fountains within,
our shadows intersect these white walls.

I couldn't resist a 600-watt light bulb wired
inside this black box. This sacred space embraces
our shadows that intersect these white walls.
Now, I wonder if my interior blurs or shines.

Inside this embrace, a black box—spaced as sacred
having felt discomforted as a woman,
You entered my honeycombed vault.
        I remember praying.
I shine my interior now, wondrous blur.

Keeping Sunrays Out

Instruction Guide for My Remains

Don't make me an urn full of ashes
only to be thrown over the bridge, or poured on the beach
where I loved to body surf, or sprinkled under the gym mats
at school where I played *Elimination* on Saturdays.
I don't want a burial near my relatives either,
or next to famous poets where taxicab drivers
will take you for free.

I want my remains cryonically frozen
in a steel chamber at Memorial Park.
I want to grimace to encourage you to run the trail,
like the skeletal grin of a wooly mammoth
I saw at a Ripley's Believe It or Not! Museum,
through a plexiglass window with cryoprotectant
chemicals pumped through my body.

I want a sprinter's position like those athletes
airbrushed on magazine covers, abdominal muscles
rippling into the next century as if to say:
my DNA will thrive after scientists solve that little issue
of tissue regeneration.

Once, someone gave me a battery-powered toy dog
with a cowboy hat and enormous floppy ears. Press
his right paw and the dog would sing Elvis Presley's
version of "Hound Dog," his hind quarters shaking
with a silver guitar red-dotted and illuminated
with hearts.

Press my button and my frozen corpse, now a miracle
of modern science, would sing the blues of keys
locked in the car at midnight. Try me again, and a
pre-recording would play in my old voice
about sweating a marathon.

See why I want the deep-freeze?
Tell people at the hamburger joint near the golf course
to listen to my message. Eat cheeseburgers and French
fries until you die, or come now with all your mustard
to train with the dogs and the ancient mammoths,
bellowing and hungry.

The Mudslingers

Stewart and Hondo are the lovers of earth
management tracked by golf carts
sparkling near high clear ground along fence
lines that clip-cut chocolate fields and dirt
roads with spin-splattered thin wheels
on planes of soaking creation driving the
chewed blades of the known down,
but below that surface,
they touch their skin, rub minerals against
their faces to become young again
beneath the undercarriage of vehicles
from chainful tractor pulls and agendas
caked amok. When the rain stops,
they begin to dance in puddles under the double
rainbow with whiskey bottles stuffed in satchels
hidden in their ballooning slickers and
turn, flow across the new light, and leap north
to convey a story of punching stuck goats
north across the Guadalupe River
and into the soft clay of your imagination.

Octopus

(to my imaginary sister)

If you want to open your box of pens
and sketch an octopus in New Zealand,
today would be an ideal time for it.

One is in an aquarium a short bicycle ride
from Napier where general admission
includes the little penguins, the oceanarium
with shark feeding at 2 p.m., or chicken fettuccine
at the Fish Bowl Café, all of which permits
no time to draw an octopus.

I forgot to mention the octopus, Inky,
rugby ball sized, escaped, slithering down
a long drainpipe, disappearing
into Hawke's Bay.

Why don't you pack your luggage and fly over here?
Open your acid-free sketch pad,
draw whatever octopus is left
behind window exhibit I, or charcoal
what Inky must have looked like, the tank ajar
at the top, the pipe running underneath the deck.

One day supported in a frame on the kitchen
window sill, or even the counter, is your drawing titled
"One Awesome Octopus" or "Inky Who Was Bored
to Death," your initials smudged as usual,
prompting mother, who always had us confused,
to stop her cooking and slam a cabinet door,
exclaiming "You did what? And where did you go?
Wait until your father comes home from work."

Ways to Love a Back Road

I love your back road but you're married.
The back road begins by loving you while standing
        in line for a ticket.
The back road washed away at Hotel ZaZa.
        You exited and therefore I love that one or both of us
        belong in a reality show.
I love the back road where you returned my Rolling Stones
        cassette tapes under my windshield wiper.
I love our back road fishing—
        how we caught nothing in our makeshift sailboat.
I love this back road until you make me crash.
I love the back road of your eyes.
I love that our back road up Stone Mountain was the Wrong Way.
        The helicopter lost us after we camouflaged with granite.
I love the back road that is running with you on Peachtree Road.
        I love our pain when we reach
        Heartbreak Hill at Piedmont Hospital.
I love the back road that is the Chattahoochee River.
        Beer is in the middle of our raft. This is parallel to
        College Initiation Byway.
I love the back road from Beaufort when we stole
        the soccer game and the homecoming cake.
        I love how my team was considered weak.
I love the back road you took with your cigarette
        and my green balloon on Saint Patrick's Day.
        I felt like a clown at a truck stop.
I love the disco taxicab driver that drove a back road
        to the Rammstein concert. I love that
        I could love Germany.
What I don't love about your back road is your eyes.
I don't love the back road
        when your heart is closed for winter.

Anonymous

I appreciate the fact that a million of you
have donned cool masks. I am well aware
of your ability to attack a computer server,
to shut down sewers, to uncover an address
of the bad cop, to hack NASA research, to occupy
Wall Street, to create not-safe work plans, to offshoot
as ghost security, to permit a voice be heard even if
the person is a monster, to retaliate against
an immigration bill, to change the very nature
of protesting, to land on the radar screen
of *Time* magazine's 100 most influential people.
But I was not aware that you reported
to Human Resources, which re-branded
as Everything People, which is Everything *but* People,
the fact I used expletive language with a co-worker,
not in my department, but who runs projects.
Without projects, I would no longer have
work. Fortunately, I am still here herding projects.
Everything *but* People deemed you not so credible
foregoing the virtual piece of paper that lands
in their play station regarding my performance.
And after all of that history, I was not aware of your
sneak attack in broad daylight into my office. You dropped
a slip of paper on my desk before Thanksgiving
that said you appreciated me as a co-worker. As if
in your gentleness, you have retracted your earlier move
against me. You even placed a piece of candy on top
of your note, the Starburst variety, tropical. When I unwrapped
the candy, it was almost as if we touched. I chewed
into the joy of your galaxy.

Houston

Tonight, driving along Richmond Avenue
trying to remember a favorite poem,
reciting a few lines,

I pass a ballroom and toss words
that land against a window or only the door.
I open the moon roof and say the darkest lines.

I stop at a red light near the Texaco and begin another stanza,
then stumble after passing the venue of the last poetry book signing—
an art gallery filled with an obbligato of oil paintings

that copies someone else's oil paintings. There is a line about stars,
but I can't see any. I forget the rest of it, then promise
to read it later, then I recall the reading at Rice.

It's the one about a workshop that critiques
a poem about a drawbridge operator,
and possibly death, and somehow a mouse.

I can't help but see how enormously
tempting traps baited with cheese must have been
for a mouse that lived near a drawbridge operator.

I see in the windshield, the drawbridge
operator above with clouds that seem like
marshmallows. And I'm the mouse scurrying below.

When I look in the rearview mirror, I'm the operator
with my fishing line nibbling—I like nibbling
better than jigging—and the mouse is brushing its teeth.

Afterwards, I see you, the operator
I love with zipped-up leather boots. I am the fish
hooked on your line, fighting you anyway.

The Midnight Run

Run with me
tighten your shoelaces
stretch across this bridge top
above the expressway
listen to crickets

toads left along Vassar
an empty fluorescent
path connects patches of houses
a string of hopeful eyes
when porch lights flicker on

breathe   exhale jasmine air
ignore the late show fuzz of the TV
inside behind the bar window
or the vacant babble above deck

toe the coast of a church sidewalk
remember the fresh-cut flower shop
We Do Weddings   We Deliver
deliver to a lover for embrace
until bulldozers snarl away

tear right to museums
paste collages for Rauschenberg
watch traffic lights   the mud
do not sidestep puddles
splash   do not despair

for what remains besides us
are restaurant laborers peddling
drunken drivers squealing their tires
dogs barking behind moonless fences
and sweat now falling   drips dripping

Jeanie

You hang quietly from the ceiling
until you hear a single frequency,
then actuating, opening the morning,
your vertebra slides, column greasy.
Toes rigid in screwed plasterboard,
you survive kingdoms of darkness, protect
unsolved golf clubs, garden tools, awards,
and unused potting soils; your bulb reflects.
But today was not better than before.
A spring broke, your foot ripped from the wall,
an electrical nerve at your neck tore.
Your twenty years droop in dismissal,
for a replacement with optical eyes,
rolling signals, a clean belt arrives.

Wrestling with Giant Anacondas

I have never wrestled with giant anacondas
in black, brown, or green color in South America
or any country actually.

It is more likely that I would be tussling
window treatments from the Natural
Roman Shade Family, black cherry bamboo
from the exotic collection,
price chart *D*.

Shipped to my home, these beasts
lay one day flat-folded
on the crooked bricks of my tropical
patio thirsty, then sucking water
from the garden hose,
ignoring their loop control.

But I lassoed them to the wall gripping
a cordless drill and bits—gifts from my father.
I macheted a way to Southland Hardware,
clawed through piles of molly bolts, self-drilling
anchors, toggle bolts, and other fasteners
for bracing to wallboard, plaster, metal, concrete,
stone, brick or tile surfaces.

My jimmied two-and-a-half-inch mounting brackets
collared these reptiles at their heads and tails!

Ah, it felt like a jungle upstairs that Saturday.
My father would be proud to know his son
has survived another one of life's hazards,
overcoming adversity,
meeting the challenge
of keeping sunrays out of a room.

So You Want to Be a Singer-Songwriter

People go to the Kerrville Folk Festival in carpools.
You pay a couple of dollars for the guitar raffle
and win, which is karma, right?

You stand on the same stage where Lyle Lovett,
Peter, Paul and Mary once played
to receive the guitar you can't play
and think you are famous—
which isn't so bad.

Lessons are plucked in Oklahoma City,
Woody Guthrie doesn't appear
during trips across the fret board,
those thin metal bars aren't rest areas
running east on I-40 to Okemah.
The steel strings migrate your fingers to Asia,
and a few years of meditation don't work,
and then you sell the guitar because you are poor.

Taking showers could improve your voice
to sing a few cover songs during happy hour
at a club with a band—
which is another chance, okay?

Balance your day job,
schedule local cities,
frequent economy motels,
breakfast in International House of Pancakes
before noon,
burn CDs, send people e-mails,
and avoid shaving your face
or traveling on anymore four-lane roads.

Click, clack, click, clack—
tell people you prefer to compose on a train.

Consider playing the drums or harmonica
after the vocals retire to the bar for beers.
Try tapping on the steering wheel of a borrowed Oldsmobile,
snap your fingers to an artist's soft, sensitive song.
Whistle tunes next to the jukebox at the diner—
the practice works well around festival campfires.

If you are not discovered there, climb a telephone pole,
ride on top of a VW microbus, hum Bob Dylan,
or cancel due to a death in the family of your goldfish.
Or if all that fails, write a poem
and read it out loud to people you don't know.

After Mac Brazel and His Ranch, 1947

What is this metallic-stick mess in the sheep pasture?
Whisper *kinda confidential-like* to the Roswell sheriff.
      Soldiers soon invade.
Debris is whisked into armored trucks. *Sure,*
a crashed weather balloon. Seen that before. Don't believe.

Soldiers stay confidential on Project Mogul.
      Wouldn't a Roswell sheriff
know? Sounds flimsy, why
believe a balloon carries a low frequency
beyond the Sierra Blancas? Worry that the wreckage

is a flimsy flying disk. Know that an alien
isn't a dummy with latex skin and aluminum bones.
UFOs wreck from beyond the Sierra Blancas.
Let them truck away the mess.
      Weather this. Or
crash.

Hiking in Big Bend National Park

or rather, solving a missing persons case in Sweden.
Not near Big Bend National Park,
much further away than usual

with a research assistant
who inked a dragon tattoo on her shoulder
and pierced ball bearings in her face.

You are hiking in the park right now
where I've never been while I magnify
old photographs and smoke in jags of snow.

Did you see the Santa Elena Canyon
where turtles spilled onto rocks in the Rio Grande
and sunned their houses in Mexico?

My plot thickened when the accused
offered me bourbon over ice. He pulled
a gun from the kitchen drawer,

and you had not returned from hiking
wherever you went, not to mention
it was past time to grill the ribeyes.

How wonderful that my assistant
swung a golf club at the evil man's face
before I suffocated from a bag over my head.

Did you extinguish your breath hiking
the Lost Mine Trail, or did one of the twenty-four
mountain lions devour you?

A canoe split in half once hauled
a 900-lb. dinosaur bone out of the park
then the canoe carried a dead body

not far from where you might have gone—
or maybe a helicopter will find you
after several hours if the pilot knew where to look.

I cleaned the bathroom after you left.
No wait, I was lying in bed watching a movie
in our Terlingua casita.

We went hiking earlier today in Big Bend
National Park. I've never smoked nor
been to Sweden, and no one ever went missing.

The Woman Who Drives a Taxicab in Afghanistan

I remember the sound of wheels
bouncing over rocks under a spotless sky.
The wheels of this car brought bags of rice,
flour, and tea. I milked goats, fed hens.
I cooked the rice and the toppings—
shalgam stew with turnip, cauliflower
with ginger. Our family was happy then
with the communists although don't tell
my mother. The wheel rims drove
fear into my body when they stopped
turning in front of the house and fearing
a husband who would prevent me from working.
Years later, when the Taliban left,
I fell in love with driving
around Mazar-i-Sharif in my flower,
a yellow and white Corolla
with seat covers woven in sparkles
and a good luck talisman dangling
in the front window.

I'm a firefly charting night,
emitting bright yellow arcs. Men threaten
to squash me with their palms in the name
of Islam. I am not afraid. They want
to capture me in their little glass jar,
punch holes in the lid for the breath,
lift me with fingers curled yellow-brown
like the inside of a spoiled peach. They touch
me to sense if I'm good enough to trade
as payment for their worst debt or for
a swap of property. I don't care. I am not afraid
of their calls threatening to snuff my light.
I do not drive for equality or tell them
I cannot be caught. I drive for my sister,

and my seven nieces and nephews.
When I've driven enough, these girls will leave
home, attend university, and work
alongside men. I will overhaul this country
with whatever ability I have. Watch every
last turn of this odometer. The government
is no longer godless, this city is a noble
shrine—its blue sanctuaries, the mosques.
Step by step, inside and out
of homes, this place will glow.

Since I'm a mechanic, I say the communists
were not bad. Literacy for women
pressed down on us, swaying corners of rusty
tribal law. I remember my sister and I drew
crazy portraits of each other with crayons—
our body parts out of proportion,
or we told jokes in front of a rain-dribbled
window without a hairline fracture. We would whisper
the communists had done right as my mother was intolerant,
who wanted them to go home disgraced.
"We will be free," my mother said, "when the Mujahideen
ride to Mazar-i-Sharif in victory." The Mujahideen
finally arrived as dirty mullah, ordering us
to cover, filtering us from travel without a male.
Yes, years later, my mother was happy when the Taliban
arrived until they shot and killed my brother-in-law.
No *risha*, no roots in red Taliban trucks.
My sister screamed, yelled,
pulled at her hair when she heard the news.
The next morning, the day of the *fatisha*,
we cooked the *Kahatm* dinner.
We wore black scarves, listened to a man's raspy
voice from a cassette player that chanted
verses from the Koran. This life is not fair,
but I'm no victim. I drive this car
because it was my brother-in-law's.

I drive its inner envelope into the streets. I work
the texture of its longer, lower lip.
I drive its yellow and white petals.

Closed Up Space

Scene I
>	Present day.

I'm off to Mexico City
on United Flight 494. The seat
in front retracts insulting my living room.
Modern day fine dining exists as shrunken
cranberries, a vanilla raspberry fig bar,
hazelnut spread splurging. Cellopaned.
Savory. Classic. A baldhead appears
like the surface of Mars. We land—
to breathe here will require H_2O
and an oxygenator.

Scene II
>	Next day.

I'm breathing in summer Earth
and the dirt of Mayan ruins on my own.
No problema. The maguey plant pools
six months of H_2O. A warrior
is sacrificed to strengthen God.
Serpents deliver the blood
and heart into the summer Earth and dirt.

Scene III
>	One week earlier. Houston. August.

I'm driving home from the theater.
The 240-volt line for the air conditioner broke.

Mr. Sparky enters (stage right) demanding $299.
Nothing happens.

Now I'm driving to Home Depot to buy
a portable air conditioning unit for $199.95.
Still sweating.

Scene IV
        One week & two hours before.

In this play, *Close Up Space*,
an editor wants to
send his daughter to boarding school.
She speaks Russian and dresses
like Lenin's daughter.
The office gopher, Steve, camps
in a Coleman two-person
tent in the office.

He feeds a goldfish swimming
in a bowl of H_2O until
no more H_2O. Gap in brain.
He meditates. Au naturel.

Fish dies. Girl leaves for Russia. Dad is sad.

Scene V
        Three weeks later.

I leave my home for the Relocated Space.

Dear Relocated Space: I know your A/C works great,
yet I would like to inquiry the status of current occupant,

Sciurus carolinensis. Last forecast reported 93% gone.
My arrival was to commence pronto. I'm concerned,

but not limited to, the possibility of contracting rabies
from the saliva of said animal. Willing to barricade doors

with luggage. When can I close up space inside?
Given all the options, can I park my Honda

in one of your appendices, an archaic wooden-covered
structure likely to scrape my side doors? I promise not to call

the police about the weed smokers. I will feed the stray cat that eats
like a horse. I am, by nature, social, and well-skilled

at utilizing methods of self-expression and exchanging
ideas. Abrazos, Homo sapien.

Scene VI
      Five weeks later.

I have been accepted by Relocated Space.
No squirrels, no dead animals, no police.
I return home cooled down.

The Archuleta Whistleblower

My name is Thomas Elwin Castello. I was the Senior
Security Technician at the base below this mesa

of elevated strangeness near Dulce, New Mexico where
a 1960s think tank developed a mole machine that melted

rock using nuclear-powered, wolfram-graphite tipped
drill cones, which located the original ice caves

and sulfur springs that aliens found perfect
especially the finished walls polished smooth as black

glass. Dungeons & Dragons fanatics
and other human workers have been the biggest

problem wandering the Off Limits area,
bottomless shafts wide enough to drive

a semi-truck through rooms emanating
a greenish phosphorescent glow

where lizard people thrived in the labyrinths.
I knew of disabled video cameras,

altered cow blood, and smuggled documents
concerning the copper and molybdenum. I speak out

only now, under penalty of death, because I learned
of an inmate with high sperm count ready to escape

rather than lose his soul before creating another
non-gender bio-form. I knew this was not

the usual hospital security job. I'm telling the truth—
I once protected research for marvelous new cures

on the surface of Earth. If you don't believe me,
ask the Apaches, or see the mutilated animals,

or touch the Autumn Joy that survive desert heat
with its fleshy leaves and scalloped margins.

The Woman Who Owned a Taxicab Company in Mexico

I

I am no strong angel,
not in my father's eyes.
I learned to forgive
him more than once.
The first time I wanted
to be a nurse,
he said, "No, look what
your older sister has done."
I said nothing—she wasted his
money on macho men instead
of her studies. She had three children,
ran away without them. How many
times can angels come back?
I worked at La Buena Vida Bakery
in San Miguel—I kneaded dough
for cinnamon buns, finished
by 8 a.m., then worked the cash register.
My father, he said, "We will raise
your sister's children." I thought how many
angels and when will they come—
I'm not the strong one. I wanted to
rewrite little pieces of paper tied
to all the balloons we sent
to the Three Wise Men from the jardin
and hoped they would listen. If not, I
imagined baking *Roscas de Reyes*,
selling them to myself, finding
the baby Jesus, all three in each cake
to swallow, to save inside my body. So I
forgave him for no nursing studies.

II

My father drove a taxi, but he could not drive
to the airport. The airport—a special license.
Federal plates, too. Taxi drivers were not happy.
A few called a meeting in secret. My father said,
"I can't go because I'm sick, so you go, Maria."
"I'm only twenty-three, I know nothing
about taxis," I replied. "No, you have to go, take
notes." "I'm pregnant," I said. I went as the only
woman. The men at the meeting said my father
was *loco*, was he really sick? I said yes, he is really
sick. They liked my English. A luxury Suburban
is required for the airport, I wrote. New or used?
Was a Suburban like a pick-up we drove
to the movies? Or was it like an elephant invited
to a quinceañera party? The meeting was like nirvana.
I had light to help my father for the first time.
When I came home, I told my husband, the carpenter,
of this new vision I could build. All he said was "Well,
it's lunchtime and I'm hungry. Fix me something."
He said a luxury Suburban is not like the pick-up
I remembered from the movies or the one he owned
to carry supplies. He showed me a Suburban one day.
I thought my dream was lost, like dough you work
that doesn't rise. No, more like the girl whose mother
says you never want to look pretty. Cut your hair
like a boy, but the girl is stolen by the narcos and never
returns. That day I felt stolen. The baby Jesus left.
What angels? My father did not go to church. When
would we ever have enough money for a Suburban?

III

"You remember that you own some land,"
my father said. "It is true," my mother added
when I asked her. "Yes, eight years ago,

you worked for your uncle
at the grocery and saved your money,"
she continued. "I suggested you buy this
land from our friends who were poor, so
you agreed to buy it from them when you
gave me the money." I never saw the land;
I was fifteen years old. The land meant nothing
then but was developed and worth ten times
what I paid. "You can haul your building supplies
and carry your gear to fùtbol games
with a Suburban," I told my husband. He was
excited then. He got rid of his pick-up. The land
was worth enough for a down payment
for a two-year old white Suburban, the very first
one in San Miguel to go to the airport. The dream
had risen like a phoenix, white and clean.

IV

No one in our family had a license to drive
the Suburban. I found a man though,
who did. He wanted to lease the Suburban
for months. "No lease," I said. What about a
commission for each fare? He agreed. We began
our Mexican marriage—we needed each other
but we didn't love each other. We could not
qualify for a cell phone account. "Let's go see
if we can take over an unpaid account," I said.
One company agreed. I printed business cards
that read: *spoken English after 3 pm.* I paid
the newspaper guy at the *jardin* to slip coupons
in *Atención*. The customers, Wilt and Rita
Fountain, did not show up at the airport once,
so the driver, the man in our marriage, offered
50% off for taking anyone back to San Miguel.
That worked. The sign for "Wilt and Rita Fountain"
was kept. After he took customers to the airport,

he held up the fake sign for a return fare
many times. I'm happy the angels didn't let us
meet the Fountains.

V

Customers wanted tours. They had no
idea where to go. I loved history. My father said,
"I give tours," yet he explained nothing,
just drove his taxi, stopped. I hired
tour guides to partner with. I said I wanted to
go with them. You cannot drive a taxi,
talk, and give a good tour. Who can? I agreed
to teach my father five new English words
a week if I did the tours. He said *duter* for
daughter. English was hardest at the mummy
museum in Guanajuato. I said *underground* for
buried, they took them up for *dug up* or *exhumed*.
I didn't know *casket*, so I said *box*. I didn't know
*a woman buried alive with hands crossed next
to her cheek*, so I said *down*.

VI

I did not learn how to drive until a rich woman
with US plates arrived with bad knees and legs.
She met my father for fares. He said to her,
"My *duter* will help you, she can provide
anything you need." He would say to me,
"You have to help her, Maria, you just have to."
"How? I am not a nurse," I said.
"You can help her," he replied.
She lived in Las Cuevitas and owned
a new chocolate Jeep. My first day of driving,
she said, "Turn on the key"
before I inserted the key in the steering column.
I steered the Jeep on the cobbled streets,

my legs shaken. The vehicle seemed broken
from the sound of *kerthud, kerthud, kerthud*.
Like a tomatillo rolling around in a boxcar.
Days began when I drove her to the doctor
or went for her medicine.

VII

My father left my mother to work
as an illegal in the US. He broke
his wrist in Arizona for a road
construction job. My mother visited him
for two weeks. She took away the remote
control for the TV that was stuck
on the Catholic channel. When my mother
returned to San Miguel, my father said,
"Forgive your husband, Maria, for his
alcohol and his womanizing ways."
He never saw my husband as good enough
for me. The Catholic channel got inside
my father. He wanted to die with all
our prayers. He was very spiritual after
the Catholic channel. He left my mother
again to fix oil pumps in Midland, Texas.
That was when he had a stroke. He died.
I was heavy inside my heart when I flew
to Midland to settle the accounting. To bring
his body back to San Miguel to bury him.
Yes, I knew *bury* and *underground*. I was not
going to cry in front of my children. I
was the strong one to show my strength.

VIII

"Yes, I can," I said when I took
my mother and my older sister
to Mexico City to buy Christmas

tree ornaments. I was seven years
old. I bought bus tickets, we had no
map, we rode Metro. I talked to
people on the streets asking
for the lowest prices. We did not
go to the popular places. I knew
I was worth something when
I returned to San Miguel, we made
a small fortune selling tin Milagros
and faceless angels made from corn husks.

IX

After my father died, I went for brain-massage therapy.
The therapist found my self-conscious part.
What I saw in my mind was myself
nine months after birth. Why then?
I could not figure this out until I realized
that was when my father came home from selling
oranges, bananas, and tomatoes
for the first time to see if he had a son.
He was not happy. He was mad and left.
My mother's mother said think of
your life, food, shelter. Like the empty
or filled glass. She said my heart is either
filled with bitterness or not.

www.ingramcontent.com/pod-product-compliance
Lightning Source LLC
Chambersburg PA
CBHW022033090426
42741CB00007B/1041